FOCUS ON™ Bio

MW01526408

Malala Yousafzai

Jennifer Strand

KAEDEN™
PUBLISHING

BOOKS IN THIS SERIES

Muhammad Ali

Neil Armstrong

Beyoncé

Jeff Bezos

George Washington Carver

Roberto Clemente

Marie Curie

Walt Disney

Thomas Edison

Henry Ford

Benjamin Franklin

Bill Gates

Jane Goodall

Mae Jemison

Steve Jobs

Bruno Mars

Barack Obama

Rosa Parks

Katy Perry

Jackie Robinson

Eleanor Roosevelt

J.K. Rowling

Charles Schulz

Maurice Sendak

Dr. Seuss

Taylor Swift

Justin Timberlake

Pharrell Williams

Wright Brothers

Malala Yousafzai

Table of Contents

Introduction

Malala Yousafzai is an **activist**. She supports girls' **rights**.

She works to help girls go to school.

Early Life

Malala was born on July 12, 1997. She is from Pakistan. Her father ran a school.

He taught Malala. She loved to read and learn.

Leader

The **Taliban** controlled Pakistan. It took away the rights of girls and women.

They were not allowed to go to school.

Malala spoke out against the Taliban.

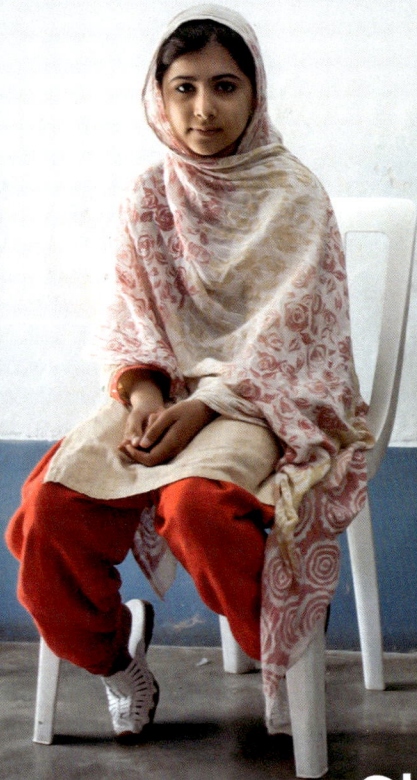

She also wrote a blog.

People around the world read it. They learned what it was like to live under the Taliban.

History Maker

Taliban members did not like what Malala was doing. They tried to stop her.

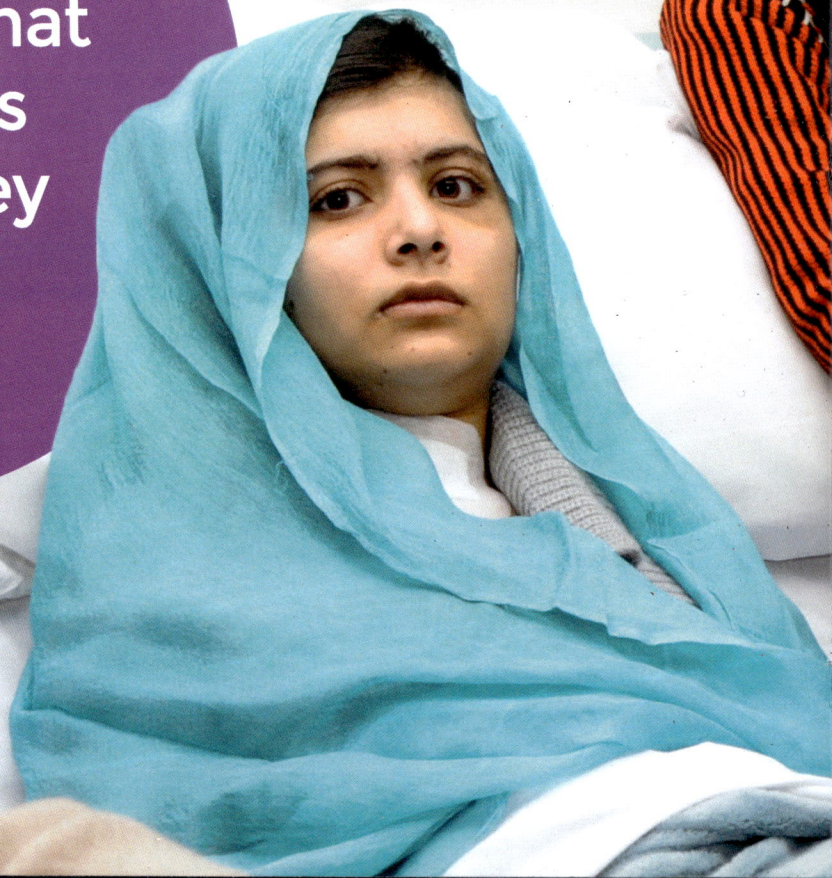

On October 9, 2012, she was shot. But she survived.

She kept speaking against the Taliban. People all over the world heard about her. So Pakistan made a new law.

It helped more children go to school.

Legacy

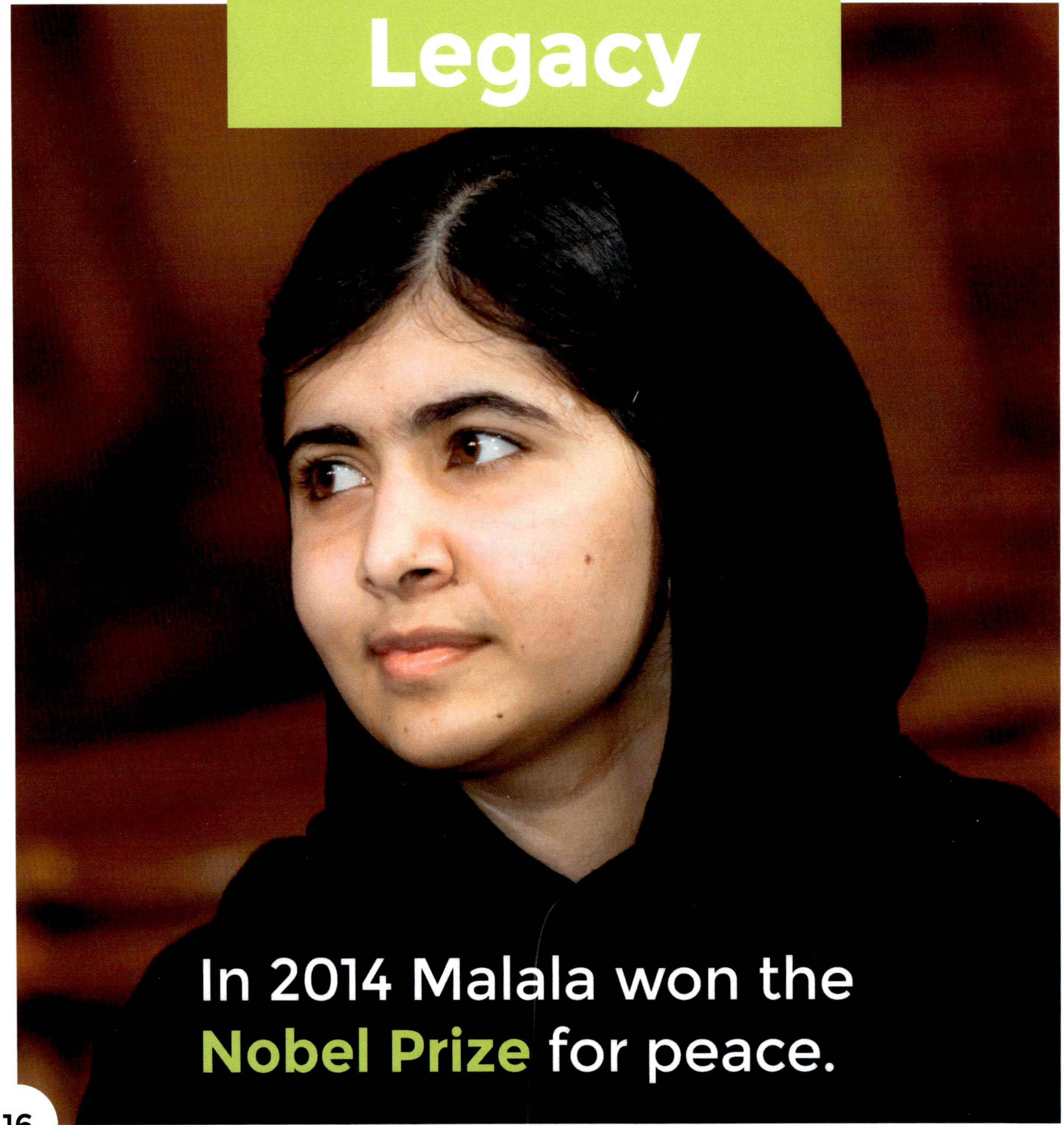

In 2014 Malala won the **Nobel Prize** for peace.

She was 17 years old. She was the youngest person to win this prize.

Today Malala is still speaking out. She works to protect the rights of girls around the world.

Malala Yousafzai

Born: July 12, 1997

Birthplace: Mingora, Pakistan

Known For: Malala is an activist. She speaks out against the Taliban. She supports education for all girls.

Key Dates

1997: Malala Yousafzai is born on July 12.

2008: The Taliban takes control of Pakistan's government.

2009: Malala begins writing a blog.

2012: Malala is attacked by the Taliban.

2013: Malala writes a book about her life.

2014: Malala wins the Nobel Peace Prize.

Glossary

activist - a person who works for change

Nobel Prize - an important award given out each year

rights - the things that people can do under the law

Taliban - a terrorist group based in Afghanistan

Index